Everything You Need to Know About

BEING A VEGAN

Vegan meals are easy to prepare once you know how.

Everything You Need to Know About

BEING A VEGAN

Stefanie Iris Weiss

THE ROSEN PUBLISHING GROUP, INC.
NEW YORK

To my brother Hal, whose love for all beings of the Earth will always be an inspiration to me: Blessed be.

I'd like to thank all the veggies who have shared wisdom, wit, and recipes with me: Ora, Liz G., Sherene, Nance (new convert!), Kiki, Rachelle, and Miss. To all the non-veggies that I love anyway: Mom, Dad, Jodi, Lynn, Liz S., and Zig. Huge thanks to my editor Erica Smith for patience and good vibes. Thanks to author and visionary Francis Moore Lappe for writing *Diet for a Small Planet,* and to the LifeThyme health food store in Greenwich Village for supplying me with organic food and smiles. More props to the Grey Dog for endless cups of coffee with SOY MILK!

Published in 2000 by The Rosen Publishing Group, Inc.
29 East 21st Street, New York, NY 10010

Library of Congress Cataloging-in-Publication Data

Weiss, Stefanie Iris.
    Everything you need to know about being a vegan / Stefanie Iris Weiss.— 1st ed.
      p. cm. — (The need to know library)
    Includes bibliographical references and index.
    Summary: Discusses the different motivations and special nutritional needs of vegans, the different kinds of vegetarianism, and ways to change to a vegan diet.
    ISBN 0-8239-2958-2 (lib. bdg.)
    1. Veganism—Juvenile literature. [1. Vegetarianism.] I. Title. II. Series.
  1999
  613.2'62 — dc21

Manufactured in the United States of America

Contents

Introduction

Nonviolence leads to the highest ethics, which is the goal of all evolution. Until we stop harming all other living beings, we are still savages.

—Thomas Edison

Human beings need to eat in order to survive. However, people often eat for a variety of reasons: because we are hungry, because we like the taste of a certain food, or sometimes even because we are bored. Very often we eat on the run. What's more, we don't always think about what we choose to eat, but that is changing.

Defining Your Diet

Meat and dairy products are a major part of the diet of North Americans. But as you'll read later, meat and dairy are not always the most healthy choices, either for your body or for the environment. More and more people are looking for alternatives.

Vegetarianism is one alternative. There are several different variations of vegetarianism, and all of them involve some form of not eating meat. Some people don't eat red meat but still eat poultry and fish. Others don't eat poultry or fish. Those who are vegetarian but still eat dairy and eggs are called ovo-lacto vegetarians. (Eggs are not officially a dairy product, although they are often considered one.)

Vegans are stricter about their diet than vegetarians: In addition to not eating red meat, poultry, or fish, they also don't eat eggs or dairy. Some people don't eat these foods because although eggs and dairy are not animal flesh, they still come from animals. Others may consider them unhealthy in light of certain conditions (such as allergies) or other dietary needs.

Beyond modifying their diet, many vegans refuse to consume any animal products. That means they do not wear leather or consume anything else derived from an animal source. As a result, people who make this choice have to carefully read the ingredient list on everything they buy, from bottled soft drinks to shampoos. However, this restriction does not necessarily apply to everyone who calls himself or herself a vegan. If you simply stop eating animal products, you can consider yourself vegan.

Why Go Vegan?

There are many reasons to go vegan. Vegans do not eat any animal flesh or consume any other animal products for both health and moral reasons.

Becoming a vegan means making a commitment to both health and moral issues.

The most commonly cited motive is to stop participating in the suffering of animals. Many vegans work actively for animal rights organizations and educate themselves about animal welfare.

Then there are those people who become vegan for health reasons. It has become apparent that eating meat and dairy products can be damaging to human animals too. Consuming pesticides, antibiotics, and genetically engineered organisms is one potential danger of eating animal products. People with lowered immunity and those who just want to improve their health are good candidates to investigate the culture of veganism.

About This Book

This book will explore all the reasons you might want to try veganism and show you how to do it. If you decide that veganism is for you, the tips you will pick up by reading this book can make your life a lot simpler.

Some people have wanted to become vegan or vegetarian for a while but they have been worried that they wouldn't be able to eat anything. That is a misconception. This book will explain to you the foods you should eat, where you can find them, and how to prepare them. Also, you will learn to anticipate the social aspects of your choice—such as dealing with parents and friends who may not understand—and discover ways to help others respect your decision.

Becoming a vegan is a serious commitment, but it is one that many people are glad they have made.

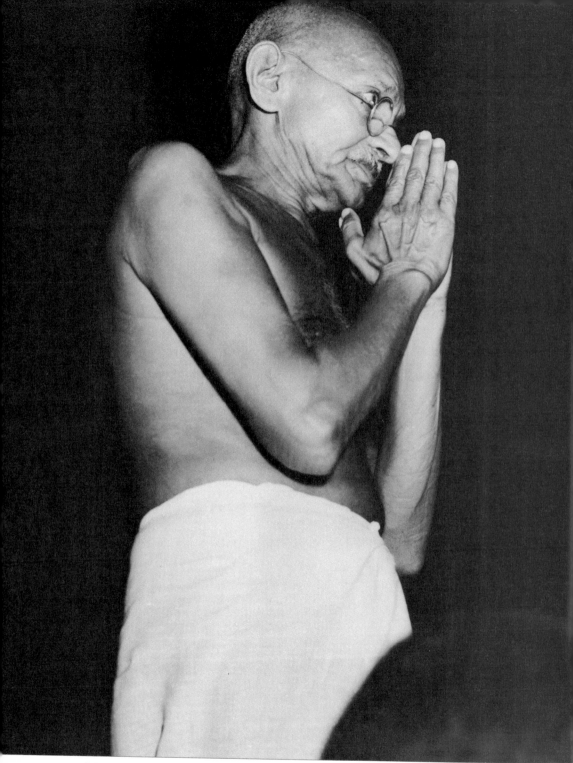

Mahatma Ghandi, who had a deep spiritual commitment to nonviolence, extended this belief to all animals, including nonhuman ones.

Chapter 1

Animal Liberation

*The greatness of a nation and its moral progress can
be judged by the way its animals are treated.*
                              —*Mahatma Ghandi*

A large part of understanding veganism is understanding the philosophy behind the animal rights movement.

Many people consider themselves animal lovers. They donate time and money to animal rights organizations and take in stray cats and dogs. Also, many people believe that no distinction should be made between the animals that are our "friends"—like cats and dogs—and animals that traditionally have been thought of as "service" animals—such as cows and chickens.

When some people begin to truly understand that animals are killed for food, or they learn of the ways in which these animals are abused before being slaughtered, they can no longer eat them. A lot of vegetarians, vegans, and other animal lovers say that one day they

The Keeping of Good *Karma*

"Karma" is an ancient Indian word that is roughly equal to the Western concept of cause and effect. If we believe in the concept of karma, we believe that every action we create will have an equal and opposite reaction. Many vegans choose their lifestyle because they want to keep their karma intact. Becoming a vegan is often the first step toward a life of humanitarian activism and service. Once you learn about what it takes to get a chicken wing onto your plate or the process of producing milk, you'll understand why people turn to veganism.

just "woke up" to the reality of animal suffering. They read a book or saw a film about animal cruelty, or they simply had a discussion with an individual who enlightened them.

Big Business

You probably have seen advertisements in magazines and on television sponsored by the meat and dairy industries. Slogans—such as "Got Milk?"; "The Incredible Edible Egg"; and "Beef: It's What's for Dinner"—promote these foods as basic necessities in our lives. But they don't have to be. Remember that as with any other commercials, these ads are sponsored by big businesses that want you to buy their products.

Nine million animals a day are slaughtered for food.

The meat and dairy products that people consume are provided by an industry called agribusiness. It is one of the most profitable industries in the United States. The places where animals are raised for food are no longer the small, family-owned farms seen on the sides of country roads in old movies. Most are large corporations, and their goal is to supply the public with the cheapest products possible.

Nine million chickens, pigs, turkeys, calves, and cows are killed in agribusiness *every day* in this country, just for food. And a lot of money is made from the consumer demand for cheap and plentiful animal products.

The conditions at agribusiness factory farms are very harsh. Animals confined in pens are almost always

Environmental contamination can harm even those animal populations that are not being raised for meat.

overcrowded, because overcrowding means increased production. The typical egg factory can hold up to 80,000 chickens, with four or five chickens squeezed into a cage that is sixteen by eighteen inches. Imagine living your entire life in a packed elevator.

These conditions have many devastating effects on animals. Chickens can become extremely agitated in the confinement of their pens and try to peck each other to death. As a result, factory farmers may cut off the chickens' beaks in order to prevent pecking. Pigs in captivity also have been known to practice self-mutilation in the form of tail biting. Calves intended for slaughter are often kept in pens so small that their muscles are unable to develop properly. This is seen as desirable because veal, the meat that comes from calves, will therefore be more tender.

Agribusiness can harm the environment as well as the animals that populate it. It takes 2,500 gallons of water to produce one pound of meat—both to feed the animal and to grow the food that the animal consumes. Water is not an endless resource, and much of the ground water left on the earth is contaminated. Factory farming also has contributed to water contamination, for a great deal of animal excrement and pesticide residue has been released into rivers.

You may gain an interesting perspective on the production of meat if you consider it alongside the realities of world starvation. Cattle raised for meat production consume enough grain to feed 8.7 billion people a year. This is double the human population of the world. Meanwhile, sixty million people starve to death each year. In theory, if we used this overabundance of grain to feed hungry people instead of raising more and more cows, we could make major strides toward ending world hunger.

How to Help

The good news is that by considering becoming a vegan, you can help the world as well as yourself. That doesn't mean you have to single-handedly end animal cruelty (although that is an admirable goal that you might pursue down the road). If you simply

On your own, you too can bring about vegan awareness.

stop consuming meat and dairy today, you *will* make a difference.

You may think, "I'm just one person—how can I possibly help?" Well, think about this: If everyone in the country responded to recycling laws by saying, "I'm just one person; it doesn't matter what I do," the environmental movement never would have made any progress. However, when many individuals decided that they would separate their trash or recycle a can instead of throwing it in the garbage, suddenly there was a recycling movement. That is why single individuals can and do change the world.

After you read this book, you might share it with a friend. Maybe you'll contact one of the organizations listed in the Where to Go for Help section, or you might even start a vegetarian or vegan awareness group at your school. Maybe you will just change your own diet. But whatever you do, the changes you make will make a difference. Over the course of your life, your decision not to eat animals will effectively *reduce the demand* for animal products. Agribusiness leaders have no choice but to listen to the voices of vegetarians and vegans. One of those voices can be yours.

Drew Barrymore, who is vegan, refuses to wear leather, suede, or fur.

Famous Voices

Did you ever notice that trends always seem to start with movie and rock stars? A lot of famous people are not afraid to express their social conscience. Drew Barrymore refuses to wear leather. Woody Harrelson wears only hemp cloth. Joe Miele poses with a vegan basketball in PETA's *Animal Times*. The Artist Formerly Known As Prince refuses to eat "anything with parents."

The hard-core music scene has embraced veganism for many years. Hard-core is a post-punk style of loud, fast music with politically oriented lyrics. "Straightedge" evolved out of the hard-core movement. Straightedgers don't drink or do any drugs. Many of them are vegan, because they refuse to put anything harmful into their bodies, as well as animal liberationists, because they oppose all forms of exploitation.

The statistics in this chapter were taken from the pamphlet 101 Reasons Why I'm a Vegetarian *by Pamela Teisler, available from Vegan Outreach. See the Where to Go for Help section at the back of this book in order to contact Vegan Outreach.*

Chapter 2

Healthy Living

Eating healthily and feeling happy with your life go hand in hand. You might be considering veganism because you want to change the world, or maybe you simply want to enjoy your *own* world a little more. Choosing a vegan lifestyle can improve your life in many ways.

First, let's look at some of the health problems caused by meat and dairy consumption. The consumption of animal products has been linked to heart disease, osteoporosis, diabetes, cancer, and arthritis. Dangerous herbicides and pesticides are more concentrated in the bodies of those who consume meat and dairy products. If a cow eats grass contaminated by pesticides and then the cow is eaten by a human, the human ingests the pesticides that are present in the

Eating the flesh of cows puts you at risk of ingesting harmful pesticides.

flesh of the cow. (Remember that this flesh contains a *lifetime* of pesticides ingested by the cow.)

Pesticides are dangerous, toxic chemicals sprayed on plants to keep them growing year-round without interference by insects. Pesticides are known to cause many kinds of cancer and other autoimmune diseases. The most common forms of cancer include those of the colon, breast, cervix, uterus, ovary, prostate, and lung. Although vegetables also may contain pesticides, meat contains approximately fourteen times the amount of pesticides of plant foods. Dairy foods contain about five and a half times the amount of pesticides of plant foods.

Another way that factory farmers try to increase meat and milk production is by giving animals antibiotics.

Herbivores lack the physical traits—such as sharp teeth and claws—of naturally carnivorous animals.

One of the most dangerous results of this practice is that humans, after regularly eating products that contain antibiotics, build up a resistance to antibiotics—which they may need if they get sick. For example, by drinking milk and eating butter, cheese, and animal flesh, you consume secondhand antibiotics. Then if you catch strep throat, your doctor will prescribe an antibiotic to cure you, but the drug may be less effective. This is because your body has built up an immunity to it.

Another dangerous additive that can be found in animal products is called Bovine Growth Hormone, or BGH. BGH is used to increase milk production in cows. Agribusiness uses BGH for the same reason that it crowds animals into small pens—for the cheapest and

Carnivore or Herbivore?

Here's a weird phenomenon: the drinking of cow's milk by humans. Human beings are the only mammal on the planet that consumes the milk of another mammal. Sounds pretty unnatural when you think about it, huh?

Furthermore, the human digestive system resembles that of an herbivore, not a carnivore. (An herbivore is a plant-eating animal, and a carnivore a meat-eating one.) Our saliva is able to digest carbohydrates more readily than it can digest meat. Our livers don't produce as much bile, the enzyme that breaks down fats found in meats, as the livers of carnivores. Also, human hands do not have claws or sharp teeth with which to tear flesh, like those of carnivores. Many vegans point to these facts as evidence that nature intended for us to have a nonmeat diet.

fastest production possible. No one knows exactly what BGH can do to human beings because its effects have not been thoroughly studied. We do know, however, that it can make cows sick. As a result, some dairies will place labels on their milk cartons stating that they do not use BGH. But it is still hard to know if BGH has been used in other products you consume. Later on, we'll discuss organic farming. Organic farmers do not use pesticides, antibiotics, or hormones.

Fat Is Not Phat

People often become vegetarian or vegan because they want to become healthier. Changing from a flesh-based diet to a plant-based diet is one effective way to help

The *Moosewood Cookbook,* a vegetarian classic, is a great place to start for meal ideas.

yourself lose weight. Meat and dairy are high in satu-
rated fat, a substance that causes the high rate of heart
disease in the United States.

Four thousand Americans also die of heart attacks
every day. Studies have shown that cholesterol, found in
animal products, is directly related to heart disease. If
your cholesterol count is elevated (above 150), you are a
candidate for atherosclerosis—the buildup of fat and
cholesterol in the arteries that blocks blood flow. But your
cholesterol level can be brought down dramatically by
switching to a vegan diet.

Other more immediate dangers of a meat-and-dairy-
based diet are salmonella poisoning, allergies, and the
susceptibility to colds and flu. Dairy also contributes to
the production of mucus in the respiratory system. If
you have allergies, reducing or eliminating your dairy
intake can help to alleviate your symptoms. Teens with
acne often find that giving up dairy and meat helps to
clear up their skin!

Try going without any dairy products for two weeks
and see if you feel any positive effects: clearer nasal pas-
sages, increased energy, clearer skin.

Whole Foods

North Americans don't get sick simply because we eat
meat and dairy. In general, our fast-food, fast-moving
lifestyle doesn't encourage mindful eating. If you really
want to be healthy, you must stop and think about what
you put into your body.

Foods made from whole grains have more nutrients than refined products, such as breads made with bleached white flour.

Many of us eat a great deal of processed food, laden with chemicals and preservatives. These foods generally are devoid of nutrients and don't contribute to good health. One important step for good health is avoiding processed foods, such as prepackaged dinners, and choosing fresh foods instead.

You also may want to rethink the foods you consider healthy. For example, foods made with bleached white flour, such as bread, bagels, and pizza crusts, are refined foods. Refined foods are not digested as whole foods, because most of the nutrients they once contained were lost in the refinement process. Better alternatives to refined foods are whole foods: brown rice instead of white rice, whole wheat bread instead of white bread,

Tofu, high in protein, is the backbone of a healthy vegan diet.

and so on. Drinking water and fresh juices instead of soda is another healthy choice.

Learn to read labels. If the label says that a product contains preservatives or artificial ingredients, try to avoid it if you are seeking to improve your health.

The Protein Myth

Skeptics of vegan and vegetarian diets will always warn you right away about the dangers of a lack of protein. The truth is there is a long and lingering myth in the Western world regarding the need for protein. We need far less than we have been told.

Protein *is* essential to health. But only 2.5 to 10 percent of our total daily calories need to come from protein. (Pregnant women should get a bit more.) You can easily get an adequate amount of protein from a vegan diet.

One of the best sources of protein is the humble soybean, which is often made into tofu. (We'll learn more about tofu in a later chapter.) Soybeans contain all eight of the essential amino acids. Amino acids are the building blocks of protein.

The chart beginning on the next page will help to assure you that adequate protein can be obtained through a vegan diet. The next time people ask you, "But what about protein?" you can just tell them that vegans can get plenty of protein.

Other Nutrients

Another common myth is that vegetarians, and especially vegans, do not get enough calcium because they do not drink animal milk or eat dairy products. Dairy products are a popular source of calcium, but they may not be the best source, especially since they are often high in fat. Vegans do have to be extra-careful to get the calcium they need, but there are plenty of ways to do so. Dark green, leafy vegetables like spinach, kale, and broccoli are excellent sources of calcium. Calcium also is found in foods such as winter squash, almonds, and some beans. Most soy and rice beverages, along with tofu and some brands of orange juice, have extra calcium added.

Iron is an important nutrient that helps carry oxygen

Vegetarian Foods	Percentage of Calories from Protein
LEGUMES	
Soybean sprouts	54%
Soybean curd (tofu)	43%
Soybeans	35%
Lentils	29%
Split peas	28%
Kidney beans	26%
Navy beans	26%
Lima beans	26%
Garbanzo beans	23%
VEGETABLES	
Spinach	49%
Watercress	46%
Kale	45%
Broccoli	45%
Brussels sprouts	44%
Turnip greens	43%
Cauliflower	40%
Mustard greens	39%
Mushrooms	38%
Lettuce	34%
Green peas	30%
Zucchini	28%

Cucumbers	24%
Green peppers	22%
Artichokes	22%
Cabbage	22%
Eggplant	21%
Tomatoes	18%
Onions	16%
Beets	15%
Potatoes	11%
Yams	8%

GRAINS

Wheat germ	31%
Rye	20%
Wheat, hard red	17%
Wild rice	16%
Buckwheat	15%
Oatmeal	15%
Millet	12%
Barley	11%
Brown rice	8%

FRUITS

Lemons	16%
Honeydew melon	10%
Cantaloupe	9%
Strawberries	8%

Oranges	8%
Grapes	8%
Watermelon	8%
Tangerines	7%
Papayas	6%
Peaches	6%
Pears	5%
Bananas	5%
Grapefruit	5%
Pineapples	3%
Apples	1%

NUTS AND SEEDS

Pumpkin seeds	18%
Peanuts	17%
Sunflower seeds	13%
Walnuts, black	12%

to the blood. Iron deficiency has long been one of the main concerns for vegetarians and vegans because the body absorbs the iron from meat faster than the iron from plants. But adding vitamin C to the diet helps your body absorb iron from plants, so this problem is easy to fix. To get iron, vegetarians choose foods like dried fruit (raisins and prunes are a great and easy choice), dark, leafy greens, legumes, and grains. Check with your doctor if you are not sure that you are getting the iron you need.

Vitamin B12 is found only in various animal products. Too little of this vitamin can cause fatigue, nerve damage, and certain kinds of anemia (a blood disorder). If you eat an ovo-lacto vegetarian diet, you will get more than enough of this nutrient. Also, it is believed that vitamin B12 is retained in our bodies for long periods of time, so if you have eaten animal products in the past, you should have enough of this nutrient to last for several years. However, it often is recommended that vegetarians—and especially vegans—take a B12 supplement or eat cereals fortified with B12 to ensure good health. Again, you may want to talk to your doctor about your health and nutritional needs as a vegan. He or she can recommend supplements and foods that will ensure complete nutrition for you.

Now you know more about both the health-related and moral reasons that people choose to become vegan. Are you considering it? You might be thinking that veganism is great for both your body and your soul. But how will veganism affect your lifestyle? Even if it is relatively easy for you to find the right foods, it is sometimes hard to convince the people with whom you share your life that you have made the right decision. In the next chapter, we'll explore how you can cope with the people who question your choices.

Veganism involves making informed choices every day about the foods you eat.

Chapter 3

Making Choices

When I was a freshman in college, I decided to be a vegan. I based my decision purely on my dedication to environmental causes. But instead of doing the proper research and asking questions, I launched headlong into my new lifestyle without knowing all of the facts.

Rather than learning how to eat balanced vegetarian meals and calmly sharing my new knowledge with my parents and friends, I embarked on a zealous campaign to convert the world to veganism. I also simply cut meat and dairy out of my life. At first I ate only bread, because I didn't know anything about preparing vegetables, tofu, and whole grains. I made this choice too rashly, and I paid for it by getting sick. I developed anemia. It gave my parents even more reason to distrust my lifestyle choice.

Eventually I learned how to be a healthy and happy vegan, and I've even shown my younger brother by

If your parents aren't vegetarian or vegan, they will probably have a lot of questions about your new diet.

example why vegetarianism is so cool. He's a freshman in college now and a member of PETA—People for the Ethical Treatment of Animals. It took years for my parents to understand my choice to stop eating animals. When I come home for holidays, they sometimes still try to offer me chicken or steak for dinner. And I have to calmly explain my beliefs to them once again. You'll have to be really patient if you decide to give up meat and dairy.

In our meat-loving culture, your choice is not likely to be welcomed with open arms. That is why it is so important for your decision to become vegan to be well researched and informed. If you don't know your facts, it might backfire on you when you approach your loved ones.

If after you have finished reading this book, you decide that veganism is for you, continue in your quest for information. Contact the organizations listed in the Where to Go for Help section. Talk to vegans and vegetarians in your school or town. Every vegetarian has a coming-of-age veggie story to tell. Hopefully yours will be a peaceful story with a happy ending!

Peace Out

Parents, guardians, and other family members might be hard to deal with at first. If they are unaware of the benefits of vegetarianism, they will question your decision. But if you approach them with well-documented information about your choice, they should have no reason to disagree. They may disagree anyway, but at least you will have shown them your reasons for becoming a vegan.

Once you've clearly explained to them your choice, you can develop a plan to maintain domestic peace. This plan probably will focus on the kitchen and the food-shopping list. Since you've made a pretty adult decision by becoming a vegan, be prepared to take on adult responsibilities. Don't expect your mom, dad, sister, or brother to be the one to figure out what you should eat. Help to make grocery lists, including the foods you need to buy. Go to the store yourself and check out what's on the shelves.

Becoming a vegan often involves finding new places to shop—such as health and bulk food stores.

Nuts and seeds are a delicious and nutritious form of portable protein.

Find out where the nearest and best health food stores are in your town. Ask questions once you get there. If you don't have a health food store near you, you can order some foods from the mail-order companies listed in the Where to Go for Help section in the back of this book.

Keep Cool

The new stuff you learn about veganism will be fascinating, and you'll probably be tempted to turn other people on to it. Be careful to spread the word in a positive way. It's tempting to get on a soapbox and shout out all the reasons why meat eating is evil. This is not a good idea—it just makes everyone around you angry.

Instead, calmly tell people about why you made your choice, and offer to give them some good reading on the subject. This is a better and more effective way to convert someone to veganism or vegetarianism than looking at his or her plate of spaghetti and meatballs and screaming, "Murderer!"

Eating Out

Another dilemma you may run into (especially if you don't live in a city or town with vegetarian restaurants) is trying to find something to eat when you are out. Depending on where you live and where you are going, you may have to adopt the habit of packing meals and snacks for yourself.

Packing meals will be a good lesson in organization for you. If you often find yourself jetting off after school without making plans in advance, it might help to prepare baggies of travel food several times a week. (Sandwich bags are one of the greatest inventions ever for a veggie on the run!) Nuts and seeds are foods commonly eaten by vegans, often in the form of little snack bars, and they are great for traveling.

You Are What You Wear

Beyond diet, many vegans attempt to eliminate *all* animal products from their lives. They refuse to wear leather, do not use any cosmetics that have been tested on animals, and actively search for nonanimal sources of consumer products.

Members of PETA, an animal rights organization, frequently protest against animal exploitation.

You might say, "How can I possibly ever wear shoes again?" Well, it's not as hard as you think. Vegan Outreach, a company listed in the Where to Go for Help section of this book, and PETA, mentioned earlier, will provide you with contact information for the growing number of stores and mail-order companies that produce products *not* made from animals.

PETA has dedicated a section of its Web site entirely to animal product alternatives. (It is called Shopping with Compassion, and you can find the Web address in the Where to Go for Help section at the end of this book.) PETA also publishes the *Caring Consumer Guide* each year. It has even more information about transforming yourself into a cruelty-free shopper.

Becoming a vegan is a huge commitment. It might be the biggest decision you've made thus far. It will affect your whole life, because both your body and mind will change once you have changed what you eat and the things with which you surround yourself. Be prepared to ruffle some feathers—and remind yourself that becoming a vegan is a choice you've made for yourself and for the planet. Even if some people give you a hard time, you will know in your heart that the outcome of your choice will be health, happiness, and maybe even a more peaceful world.

By now we've investigated the reasons to become vegan and some of the obstacles that new vegans face. Next we will explore some of the other nonmeat alternatives to veganism.

Chapter 4

Checking Out Other Alternatives

If you are not quite ready to become vegan but want to investigate other ways to heal your body, clean up the environment, and protect animal rights, there is a lot you can do. Many people become vegans gradually. They start by giving up poultry and beef, then give up fish, and eventually stop eating dairy products. Other people make a clean break and go cold turkey (pun intended). But if you want to take it slow, here are some ways to do so.

Several chapters ago we introduced the concept of organic and free-range farming. An organic farm uses no pesticides, hormones, or antibiotics. This includes spraying vegetation with chemicals or injecting animals with hormones.

There is a lot of controversy surrounding the rules that

govern organic farms. California was one of the first states to create laws pertaining to organic farming. Most other states are still unregulated. It's hard to be sure that a product is truly organic if it comes from an unregulated state. One way to make sure that organic farms are truly organic is by writing the farm in question and asking for literature about its practices. If it isn't too far away, go visit. You can find the phone numbers of manufacturers on product labels, or ask the clerk in the store where you go food shopping. If your local supermarket doesn't carry organic foods, explain that you want them.

The customer is always right, and in this case you will be helping to increase the demand for organic foods.

Where Is the Freedom in Free-Range?

Choosing to eat organic fruits and veggies is not that controversial, and we can be sure that they are a pretty good bet healthwise. But what if you're not quite ready to give up dairy and eggs? What does the term "free-range" really mean?

Laws don't really exist yet to govern so-called free-range farms. According to PETA, many free-range farms simply keep their chicken pens unlocked, but the laying hens are still subjected to abusive practices. The chickens are not hanging out happily in the sunshine laying eggs on their own time. They often are still molted—starved to stop them from laying eggs for a few months. Molting is done to control egg prices.

Free-range animals are rarely treated much better than factory-farmed ones.

"Free-range" often only means that animals have some limited access to the outdoors. They are not necessarily protected from harm. Many of these farmers claim that their animals are given organic feed, which is supposedly for the benefit of the human consumer. But if you're considering vegetarianism or veganism because you want to stop harming animals, you need to do a lot of checking before you accept free-range products. Again, contacting and/or visiting a free-range farm might help you to decide.

Macrobiotics

Different cultures have been experimenting with various forms of vegetarianism for thousands of years.

One of the most interesting forms of vegetarianism is called macrobiotics. It is based on the Chinese concept of yin and yang, or balance. Some foods are thought to be more yin and others more yang. This diet consists mainly of whole foods. Macrobiotics are allowed to eat small portions of fish. Each meal must contain a balanced amount of proteins, carbohydrates, and fats.

Many macrobiotics try to eat seasonally. They attempt to eat only the foods that grow in their climates at particular times of the year. For instance, a person living in the northeastern United States would avoid avocado, a tropical fruit. Instead he or she would eat pumpkins, apples, and pears during the autumn harvest. People who live in cities often rely on local green markets to find locally grown, seasonal produce.

There are many other food movements that one can explore. There is pescatarianism, a variation on vegetarianism in which fish is eaten, but no other meat or dairy is consumed. There is the "living" or "raw food" movement. People who advocate the living foods movement eat only uncooked fruits, vegetables, and seeds. They believe that cooking food destroys its life force and renders it worthless. They eat many kinds of sprouts and drink a beverage called wheatgrass juice. Wheatgrass is a powerful green drink that is extracted from the wheatgrass plant in a juicer. Many people recovering from serious diseases turn to this diet to help heal themselves.

No matter what diet you choose, it is important to have a healthy balance of nutrients.

Now we know more about the history and philosophy of veganism, and some other ways to get animals off our plates. But once we have decided to eliminate animal products, what do we eat? The next chapter will show you how to create delicious, nutritious, and simple meals.

Chapter 5

Let's Get Cooking!

Hungry yet? Vegan cooking is a universe unto itself. You might think that it will be disappointing to give up pizza and hamburgers. But the food you will be eating is going to taste even better. And if you still really want pizza or burgers, you can eat soy cheese pizza (with a whole wheat crust) or veggie burgers to your heart's content.

The first and most important food to learn about as a vegan is tofu. Tofu is a substance made of fermented soybeans. It contains complete proteins. It is white and moist and looks a bit like cheese. It absorbs the flavor of anything you season it with. You can toss it into soups or salads, bake it, broil it, fry it, or eat it hot or cold, with any sauce you want. It is the best replacement for meat available.

Many different kinds of veggie burgers are widely available, and they are all very easy to prepare.

Say you really loved sesame chicken from your local Chinese restaurant. Try sesame tofu instead! Cook the tofu with the same ingredients you would have used with chicken. There are tofu hot dogs and veggie burgers made with soy. Ask the people in the health food store or local food co-op about their tofu selection. It is bound to be endless.

Another really important vegan substitute for an animal product is soy milk. Soy milk also is derived from the soybean. You can use it in any recipe that calls for cow's milk. The best thing about soy milk is that it comes in flavors like vanilla, carob, almond, and chocolate.

Try soy milk over your favorite cold cereal for breakfast. Or try instant organic oatmeal with some fruit. All you

Soybeans are used to make soy sauce, tofu, and soy milk.

have to do is boil water, pour it over a package of oatmeal, and add fruit and soy milk to sweeten it. Voila! Eating this is a hot, hearty, and healthy way to energize your day.

Other foods enjoyed by vegetarians and vegans are seitan, tempeh, and textured soy protein. All of these foods can be found in natural foods stores and vegetarian restaurants. Remember the discussion of whole foods from chapter two? The principles of whole-food eating should guide you as you shop. Make sure your breads and pastas are whole and unrefined. They also should be preservative-free. (The PETA Web site has an extensive list of preservatives.) Now let's check out some easy recipes that you can whip up and serve to your friends and family.

You'll need about a half hour to make Insta Beans and Rice.

Insta Beans and Rice

- 1-1/2 cups of instant brown rice
- 1/2 tablespoon of olive oil
- 1/4 cup of chopped onion
- 2 cloves of garlic, minced
- 1 can of pink or black beans (salt-free and organic, if possible), rinsed
- cayenne pepper, black pepper
- half a tomato, chopped

1. Cook rice according to package directions. (It usually takes about 20 minutes to make instant rice.)
2. Five minutes before the rice is done, sauté in a large skillet the garlic and onions in olive oil until the onions turn light brown, stirring constantly.
3. Add beans to the sautéed garlic and onions; stir

Wow your friends with the Greatest Guacamole Ever!

until beans are hot and everything is well mixed.
Add the spices.

4. Pour the rice into a bowl and fluff. Pour the beans
over the rice and garnish with chopped tomatoes.

Greatest Guacamole Ever

- 2 ripe avocados, peeled and pitted (ripe avocados, soft yet firm)
- 1/2 cup of chopped onions
- 4 cloves of garlic, minced
- one bunch of fresh cilantro, washed and chopped
- dash of cayenne pepper
- 1/2 teaspoon of chili powder
- 1 lemon
- half a tomato, chopped

1. In a large bowl, mash the avocados.
2. Add onions, garlic, and cilantro; mash some more. Add spices; mash again. Add the juice of the lemon, making sure not to let the seeds fall in; mash again.
3. Finally, add the tomatoes and stir gently, so as not to crush them.
4. Serve guacamole with whole-grain chips. Or serve as a side dish with Insta Beans and Rice—you have made a gourmet meal in less than 45 minutes!

Baked Tofu

- 1/4 cup of olive oil
- 2 pounds of firm tofu, drained (pat dry with a paper towel)
- scallions, washed
- 5 cloves of garlic, minced
- soy sauce

1. Preheat oven to 375°.
2. Pour olive oil over the bottom of a large baking pan.
3. Cube tofu (cut into squares). Distribute the tofu evenly in pan.
4. Drizzle lightly with soy sauce, using enough to get every piece. Sprinkle scallions and garlic over tofu so each cube is covered.
5. Cook tofu for one hour, drizzling a little more soy sauce on the tofu every 20 minutes or so.

Groovy Greens
- 1 tablespoon of olive oil
- 1/2 onion, chopped
- 1/2 teaspoon black pepper
- 1 bunch of broccoli, washed and chopped
- 1 bunch of asparagus, washed with stems cut off
- cilantro or spice/herb of your choice

1. Sauté onion and black pepper in olive oil.
2. Add broccoli; wait one minute. Add asparagus. Add other spices. Cook until veggies are just a bit brighter green than they were when raw.
3. Serve with brown rice and baked tofu.

Apple Fantasy
- 1/3 cup of brown rice syrup or other liquid sweetener
- 1/4 cup of unsweetened pineapple juice
- 2 1/2 cups of grated red apples, cored and partially unpeeled
- 1 1/2 tablespoons of lemon juice
- 1 cup of shredded, fresh pineapple
- 6 large, fresh strawberries, sliced

1. Combine rice syrup and pineapple juice in a bowl; stir well.
2. Add all other ingredients except the strawberries to the liquid; mix. Let stand for a few minutes and mix again.

Apple Fantasy tastes great over granola or all by itself.

3. Divide fruit mixture into four bowls; garnish with strawberries. Serve immediately. Pretty, tasty, easy, and healthy!

One of the great things about changing your diet is that you have a new reason to be creative. Try not to think about this lifestyle change as a painful challenge. Instead, look at it as a new opportunity. You are not really giving anything up. Instead you are inviting health, wellness, happiness, and world peace into your life and spreading peace throughout the world.

Glossary

anemia A condition that affects red blood cells. Anemia is generally caused by nutritional problems such as too little iron in the diet. People with anemia are sometimes pale and weak.

calcium A substance that is needed for the development and maintenance of healthy bones. Calcium is found in dairy products and dark green vegetables.

carbohydrate An essential nutrient that we get from many foods, including fruits, vegetables, and grains.

carotene A nutrient that is found in many fruits and vegetables and is believed to help prevent some types of cancer.

cholesterol A substance that occurs naturally in our bodies and is also found in certain foods. A high level of cholesterol in the body can lead to heart disease and other health problems.

factory farm A large farming operation, usually owned by a company rather than an individual, that produces very large quantities of farm products. Most of the meat and dairy products sold in the United States are produced by factory farms.

fiber A substance found in some foods that helps keep the digestive system healthy.

free-range Animals raised for consumption that may have been allowed some access to the outdoors.

karma Cause and effect.

legumes A group of plant foods that includes peas, beans, and peanuts.

macrobiotic A diet and lifestyle based on the Asian principles of yin and yang.

nutrient A substance found in food that helps our bodies remain healthy.

pescatarian A person who eats fish and seafood but no other animal flesh.

pesticide A dangerous chemical sprayed on produce to eliminate insects.

protein An essential nutrient that we get from certain foods, including meat, dairy products, tofu, and beans.

seitan A mixture of wheat flour, vegetable extracts, and seasonings that is used as a meat substitute.

tempeh Fermented soy with a texture similar to meat and a nutty flavor.

tofu A food made from soybeans that has a soft, cheeselike texture. Also called bean curd.

vegan Usually refers to a diet free of all animal products including dairy products; can sometimes mean a lifestyle totally free of animal products.

vegetarian A person who does not consume animal flesh.

For Further Reading

Davis, Gail. *So Now What Do I Eat?: The Complete Guide to Vegetarian Convenience Foods*. Corrales, NM: Blue Coyote Press, 1998.

Ferber, Elizabeth. *The Vegetarian Life: How to Be a Veggie in a Meat-Eating World*. New York: Berkley Publishing, 1998.

Gellatley, Juliet. *The Livewire Guide to Going, Being, and Staying Veggie!* North Pomfret, VT: Trafalgar Square, 1997.

Klavan, Ellen. *The Vegetarian Factfinder*. New York: Little Bookroom, 1996.

Marcus, Eric. *Vegan: The New Ethics of Eating*. Ithaca, NY: McBooks Press, 1998.

Null, Gary. *The Vegetarian Handbook*. New York: St. Martin's Press, 1996.

Stepaniak, Joanne. *The Vegan Sourcebook*. Los Angeles: Lowell House, 1998.

———— and Suzanne Havala. *Vegan Vittles: Recipes Inspired by the Critters of Farm Sanctuary*. Summertown, TN: Book Publishing Company, 1996.

Vegetarian Times. *Vegetarian Times Vegetarian Beginner's Guide*. New York: Macmillan, 1996.

Wasserman, Debra, and Reed Mangels. *Simply Vegan: Quick Vegetarian Meals*. Baltimore, MD: The Vegetarian Resource Group, 1995.

Where to Go for Help

Vegan, Vegetarian, and Animal Rights Organizations

American Vegan Society
501 Old Harding Highway
Malaga, NJ 08328
(609) 694-2887

People for the Ethical Treatment of Animals (PETA)
51 Front Street
Norfolk, VA 23510
(757) 622-PETA [7382]
e-mail: info@peta-online.org
Web site: http://www.peta-online.org

Vegan Action
P.O. Box 4353
Berkeley, CA 94704
(510) 548-7377
e-mail: info@vegan.org
Web site: http://www.veganorg.com

Vegan Outreach
211 Indian Drive 2
Pittsburgh, PA 15238
(412) 968-0268
e-mail: vegan@veganoutreach.org
Web site: http://www.veganoutreach.org

The Vegetarian Resource Group
P.O. Box 1463
Baltimore, MD 21203
(410) 366-8343
e-mail: vrg@vrg.org
Web site: http://www.vrg.org/

Viva Veggie Society
P.O. Box 294
Prince Street Station
New York, NY 10012-0005

Vegetarian Food and Products

Dixie Diners' Club
Dixie USA, Inc.
P.O. Box 55549
Houston, TX 77255
Web site: http://www.dixiediner.com
Soy products, Stevia (a natural sweetener), and candy.

Ener-G Foods
P.O. Box 84487
Seattle, WA 98124-5758
(800) 331-5222
e-mail: heidi@ener-g.com
Egg substitutes, rice baking mix, and other products for
people with special dietary needs.

Lumen Foods

409 Scott Street
Lake Charles, LA 70601
(800) 256-2253
e-mail: LumenFoods@aol.com
Web site: http://www.soybean.com
Soy "meats," powdered soy milk, and more.

The Mail Order Catalog

P.O. Box 99
Summertown, TN 38483
(800) 695-2241
Texturized soy protein, gluten mix, vegetarian broth, nutritional yeast, and cookbooks.

Pangea

7829 Woodmont Avenue
Bethesda, MD 20814
(301) 652-3181
Fax: (301) 652-0442
Web site: http://www.pangeaveg.com/contact.html
Vegan clothing and accessories.

Puritan's Pride

P.O. Box 9001
1233 Montauk Highway
Oakdale, NY 11769-9001
(800) 645-1030
Vitamins and nutritional supplements; good sales and prices.

Vegetarian Shoes
Web site: http://www.vegetarianshoes.com
Extensive selection of animal-friendly footwear.

Walton Feed, Inc
135 North Tenth Street
P.O. Box 307
Montpelier, VT 83254
(800) 269-8563
Web site: http://www.waltonfeed.com
Flavored texturized vegetable protein, storage foods, and food grinders.

Magazines

Vegetarian Times
For subscription information:
(800) 829-3340 or (904) 446-6914
Web site: http://www.vegetariantimes.com

Veggie Life
P.O. Box 440
Mt. Morris, IL 61054-7660
Send $23.94 for a full-year subscription. Outside of the United States, add $6.00.

Index

About the Author

Stefanie Iris Weiss has been a vegetarian for ten years. She lives in New York City (because there are awesome vegetarian restaurants there) with her nonvegetarian cat, Caboodle.

Photo Credits

Cover image & pp. 2, 8, 16, 24, 34, 36, 48, 50, 54 © Thaddeus Harden; p. 10 © AP/ Wide World; pp. 14, 38 © FPG; p. 18 © The Everett Collection; pp. 13, 21, 22, 44 © Uniphoto; pp. 26, 27, 46, 51 © Stockfood America; p. 40 © PETA